Echoes in the Everyday

Anoushka Vishwanathan

BookLeaf Publishing

India | USA | UK

Echoes in the Everyday © 2024 Anoushka
Vishwanathan

Presentation by *BookLeaf Publishing*

Web: www.bookleafpub.com

E-mail: info@bookleafpub.com

ISBN: 9789363302716

First edition 2024

To Amma

you're my role model, my inspiration, and my
best friend

LYTMLY

ACKNOWLEDGEMENT

I would like to thank my Amma and Appa, my little sister Meera, and my dog Rigby, whose unwavering support and love have been the foundationnof whatever I do.
Thank you for always being there for me, through every high and low, and for believing in me even when I doubted myself. Your support has not only nurtured my creativity but also provided the strength and motivation to continue pursuing my passions.

PREFACE

In this book, you won't find a unifying theme or structure. Instead, you'll discover a series of glimpses into my heart and mind—snippets of joy, sorrow, reflection, and wonder. The poems are born from everyday moments, each one a testament to the power of finding meaning in the mundane.

As you read through these pages, I hope you find echoes of your own experiences and emotions. May the words resonate with you, bringing comfort, insight, or simply a moment of pause amidst the chaos of daily life.

Rain's Refrain

The rain wipes everything anew,
a heavy downpour through and through,
it starts within my spire and rattles my mind
washing the dirty while keeping the kind
It reaches the crevices where my secrets lie,
to cleanse the mind and purify.
A fresh start summoned by the beat,
of raindrops where the earth and sky meet.
They fall unsure of where to go,
each cycle brings a new display.
They're forced to shift, to bend, to sway,
yet in their song, they find their way.
Down, down, down they gently glide,
only to rise with the changing tide.
But know that in their soft refrain,
a new home forms for all again.

BROWN SKINNED GIRL

brown skinned girl dreaming
hopes and aspirations fly
a mere whisper in the wind,
can make her hear both sing and die
up up and away she goes
again! again! she whispers
her head says no
while her heart screams
yes! yes! yes!
carried by her long plaits of black
lotus flowers wedged between the cracks
she's an ethereal spirit, blessed by the gods
while she has much to learn, to unpack
spirit is not one she lacks
the oldest of her kin, she burdens
while the children can sleep, uncertain
no hopes lie on their shoulders
as long as the aunties can
squeeze
smother
warm them from a world becoming ever colder
no worries, brown skinned girl says
thinks
wonders
hopes

no one can shove
cram
belittle
her big beautiful mind into dark corners
unrecognizable and unseen
into the spaces between
The American Dream
something she will never understand
an immigrant mentality
the cave
to suffice
give in
give in
GIVE IN!
no, she thinks
i can make my own world, my own mold
far from being on her forever brink
she won't do as she's told
a sea of white
suddenly she's surrounded
her heart stills, now bounded
sadness?
anger?
no, No, NO
she drowns ashamed, a deadly sin
beautiful beautiful brown skinned girl
too pure, too naive for this harsh cruel world
why are you trying to unlearn all you've been
told?

why are you hiding?
come out! come out!
you're lovely inside and out
i scream
i shout
i stomp about
brown skinned girl don't hide
please don't cower,
your black hair doesn't make you more sour
your skin glows, it's a palace- a tower!
don't listen to them brown skinned girl,
i beg
i hope
i plead
it doesn't work, my heart starts to bleed
brown skinned girl hides her hands behind her
dress
woven and sewn by her mother from hands that
never rest
brown skinned girl doesn't want to be special
anymore
she doesn't want to shine
to glow
to light
brown skinned girl please don't hide your bright
for others who will never understand your plight
brown skinned girl please listen, i beg
don't let that fire kindling in your litter chest
become the anger that destroys

that wrecks
burns all that you keep close to your heart
brown skinned girl i say,
kindle it into the flame that you are
for you are me
and i am you
brown skinned girl don't let them take
take
take
for the very part of you that is cherished
will slowly fade away
you will long
you will ache
so brown skinned girl please, for my sake
don't lose sight
be strong and brave
may you shine your bright, may you never cave
i know you've been told to keep your spirit
locked within
that to hope is but a deadly sin
but don't let those words get to your head
as from there they will grow, they will blister
what was then living, now dead
brown skinned girl dreaming
brown skinned girl screaming

Unfinished

Unfinished we are,
Climbing down down down
The steps of defeat
Scared we're going to repeat
The footsteps the ones before us made.
The wrongs the rights the inbetween
The turns the tumbles,
No chance left to redeem
Unfinished.

Not broken nor crumbled
Not battered or bruised
Simply unfinished
Our pride easily diminished
Not proud of what we left behind us
But proud of what we can be
Unfinished.

A world left divided
Arguments one sided
True selves confided
Honesty unprovided
No one united
Unfinished.

Too many challenges not overcome
The right the left the inbetween
The stabs to our self esteems
We hold these truths to be self evident
Unquestionable not debatable
Until someone dismisses them as irrelevant
Unfinished.

We hold faith in the ones in power
Regard them as the men of the hour
Allow them to overpower
Unfinished.

I look ahead of all of this.
This too shall pass
I hope we can surpass it.
Come so far from where we were
My ancestors applaud
Yet humanity's still flawed
Unfinished.

Mosquito Bites

The worst kind of pain is a mosquito's bite,
a searing itch that burns inside,
a sensation that makes your skin too tight.
You scratch, you pull, you plead for days,
a sting that lingers till morning's light.
And all for what? A tiny bump,
a fragile mark, so small, so slight,
yet no one sees the torment you hide.
I promise I'm hurting,
I promise the pain,
but with nothing to show,
I'm met with disdain.
I promise I'm sad,
though my tears aren't clear,
I promise I'm mad,
but all you see are my fears.

Echoes in Eternity

Do you ever wonder how small we are?
They say we're mere specks of dust by far,
straining our lives to reach a bar,
that doesn't exist, just out of sight,
we fight through our days, our strength ajar.

We push and we pull, we toil and trade,
hoping to leave a mark we've made,
yet the world keeps turning, unfazed by our
scars,
and life moves on, as it always has,
while we chase the distant, fading stars.

We're caught in a race, we're bound to compete,
but the finish line's lost, a deceptive feat.
We climb and we stumble, yet never complete,
the goals we set, the dreams we spin,
in a universe vast, where we're obsolete.

But perhaps it's in the striving, the endless
chase,
in the moments of joy, in the love we embrace.
For though we're small, and time's fleeting pace,
leaves barely a trace of the lives we've known,
we find meaning in each step, in every place.

So wonder we might, at how small we may be,
yet in our smallness, we find infinity.
In each heart's rhythm, in each soul set free,
we carve our own paths, no matter how thin,
and leave behind echoes in eternity.

The Onion's Lament

Beneath the blade, the onion weeps,
A silent sorrow, sharp and deep.
Its layers peel, revealing pain,
In every tear, a memory slain.

Yet in its grief, a truth is known,
That every cut brings warmth to home.
So though it wounds, we bear the sting,
For in its tears, our hearts find spring.

Between Heatbeats

Hope is that flutter in your chest,
Begging, pleading, never at rest.
Hope is rash, it doesn't think twice,
Promised words vanish like ice.

Hope won't wait for you or another,
It's a restless storm—take cover.
Hope is beautiful, hope is kind,
I find it even in my despairing mind.

Hope is the seconds that quietly pass,
Between heartbeats, between every glance.
It's the dawn breaking after the night,
A fragile thread pulled too tight.

Hope is the whisper that defies the roar,
A tiny seed that asks for more.
It's the light that seeps through the cracks,
A force that time and sorrow lack.

Hope is the hand that reaches out,
When you're drowning in a sea of doubt.
It's the strength found in a broken heart,
A promise that we'll never part.

Hope is the dream that refuses to fade,
A fire that burns in the deepest shade.
It's the courage to take one more stride,
With hope, you'll always find guide.

The Flame's Dilemma

Oh candle in the night
please tell me how you burn so bright
even in the darkest of storms
the blackest of shadows
the quietest of whispers
you still manage to shine

Is it a gift or a forever struggle?
Tell me, are you afraid
Of being steadfast and unmoved?
Do you rage if you can't escape?
Do you pick fight if you cannot fly?
What if the wax you were given
Melts away with time's passing by

And if a breath of relief becomes your last light,
And your glow fades with the sigh of night,
Will you still shine, steadfast and true,
Or surrender to the dark that grew?

The City's Burden

I wonder if the city that never sleeps gets tired.
Does it long for the quiet of the night
the whispers of a pitch black sky
to hear the wind instead of voices
natures call replacing passerby
to be a beacon instead of a desire
a symbol to admire
does it want a placid life
one without the soul crushing hours
and the people who claim to have power
does it dream of sunny days and simple nights
a life without an endless plight
I wonder if the city that never sleeps
has secrets it doesn't want to keep

Me Myself and I

In the hazy morning light
the time of day where the sun doesn't know
whether to come out or call back night
i take the time to stare into your eyes
two eyes stare back
inspecting
i see beyond the colors of brown and black
i see beyond the words you might lack
there is something unspoken between us
not quite tension but a need to discuss
for my mind is muddled and heart confused
i ask, why do u feel so used?
My body is tired and my mind is sore
i keep staring at the mirror on my bedroom floor

At the Edge of it All

If the world was flat I wonder,
If at the edge of it we would jump or admire
would we forget life's problems
and turn to our true desires
when given an option to flee or discover
would I want to know what lies beyond?
a pit of hollow nothingness
or meaning in which I find an urge to respond
would I cower and whimper
would I say its not true
that there are more things that my mind
hasn't set out to do
would i expand my heart, my soul, my essence
to find my true depth in fear's presence?
at the edge of the world would I finally shout
my heart, thoughts, and feelings out
would I be courageous and true
or is that just because everyone else is too?

The Fire Within

Passion
I feel it in my bones, it burns, it thrives,
In the depths of my mind, where my spirit
strives.
I feel it in each step, in the goals I chase,
In every change I make, in my mirrored face.

It courses through my veins, a fire untamed,
Guiding every action, leaving nothing unnamed.
In the quiet of the night, it whispers low,
A force within me that refuses to let go.

I feel it in the dawn, as dreams unfold,
In the stories I tell, in the truths I hold.
It's in the way I rise after every fall,
A relentless drive, answering passion's call.

It's there in the struggle, in the victories won,
In the battles I fight until the day is done.
I see it in my eyes, reflecting the flame,
A passion so fierce, it cannot be tamed.

A Safe Place

I drift through the heart of my bedroom's space,
Seeking comfort in corners, a quiet embrace.
Dusting off echoes of days long gone,
Erasing the traces where memories have drawn.

Birthday cards, photographs, secrets they keep,
Stashed in the eyes of my room, where shadows
sleep.
The first book I loved, the first drawing I made,
Tucked in the folds where time hasn't swayed.

These walls, they hold more than just wood and
stone,
They cradle the moments that made me, alone.
In the stillness, I find what I've left behind,
Pieces of a story, in the silence confined.

Scent of a Distant Self

A scent drifts by, familiar yet strange,
Pulling me back to a time I can't change.
It clings to the air, a ghost of the past,
A memory I thought would never last.

I'm taken to a place I barely know,
Where shadows of a former self grow.
The person I see, lost in the haze,
Is someone I was in those distant days.

The smell of regret, sharp and clear,
Brings back a time I'd rather not near.
It's bittersweet, this haunting refrain,
A melody of moments soaked in pain.

I don't recognize who I used to be,
A stranger in a life that isn't me.
The nostalgia bites, it's not the kind
That brings you peace, but leaves you blind.

I turn away, trying to escape,
But the scent lingers, altering my shape.
It's a reminder that time can be cruel,
That even a smell can make you feel a fool.

Secondhand Pages

I found it tucked away, forgotten and worn,
A secondhand book, its cover forlorn.
The spine cracked with stories it keeps,
Whispering secrets in the silence it sleeps.

I wonder who held it before it was mine,
Who traced these pages, line by line.
Did they pause at a phrase, lost in thought,
Or linger on passages that time forgot?

Their fingerprints fade, but echoes remain,
In the creases and folds, in the ink-stained grain.
Did they turn these pages with unquestionable
care,
Or in moments of sorrow, when life seemed
unfair?

Were they moved by the words, did they laugh,
did they weep?
Did this book guard their dreams, in the dark
where they sleep?
I trace the margins where they might have
penned
A note or a thought, like a message to send.

But the pages stay quiet, no answers to give,
Just the ghosts of emotions that once might have
lived.
I close the book gently, with a sigh and a stare,
Wondering who read it last, and what we might
share.

Dreamlike

I slip in and out of sleep
a mindless state
only to find my mind has been wiped of its slate
darkness's emerges and light cowers
pushed out of the spotlight, suddenly sour
my mind wanders to places I may not go
forbidden, hidden, by the only world I know
something flickers and awakes with a glow
I want to see more so I open my eyes
but i'm awaken by morning's angry light

Never Truly Silent

Has the world ever truly been silent?
Maybe when I'm sleeping,
Or maybe when I'm alone.
But I can still hear the AC humming,
And the ringing on my phone.
I can hear the crickets chirping,
And the wind moan.

Even in the stillest hours of the night,
There's a whisper in the dark, a distant light.
The creak of the floorboards beneath my feet,
The soft ticking of a clock that never skips a
beat.
A car passing by, its engine a low drone,
Reminding me that I'm never truly alone.

Even my thoughts make their subtle noise,
Echoing in my mind, drowning out the void.
So I wonder, as I lie in bed,
Has the world ever truly been silent,
Or is it just quiet instead?

A Life in the Shadows

When I was younger I wanted to see
if my shadow could move without me
I spent hours stirring and flailing
trying to catch it off guard, and failing
I kept still and stared
wondering if my shadow would twitch
or even look back at me to glare
maybe the shadow loved me too much
to ever part or expect me to share
that's why it followed me everywhere
copying my style and hair

Stargazing

When we look up at the moon
do you see the same one as me?
do you see it with a cloudy night
or stars that shine spectacularly bright
do you see after a rainy day?
when lightning has struck
and tea is made
or maybe it's hidden under the fog
that makes moonlight fade
and memories stay
I hope you look at the moon
and think of me while you do,
for we are under the same sky,
no matter the shade of blue

Echoes of Innocence

Sometimes I want so much,
And other times I simply long,
To return to a state of innocence,
When life felt effortlessly strong.

I yearn for those days of carefree ways,
When the world was bright and new,
When worries were distant, fleeting shadows,
And dreams felt vibrant and true.

My heart now seeks a deeper meaning,
In places where it might not be,
Longing for a sense of purpose,
That perhaps was never meant for me.

Yet the echoes of those simpler times,
Whisper softly in the breeze,
Reminding me of a time when life
Was lived with such easy ease.

The Final Embrace

I wonder how it feels to know,
When it's your final embrace,
Between the person you love the most,
And the tender warmth of their space.

Are there memories wrapped within your arms,
Or words left forever unsaid?
Is there a lingering unspoken sorrow,
For dreams that remained unread?

Do you hold them tightly,
To stave off the ache of their departure?
Or is it a swift, fleeting gesture,
So the memory can quickly close and fracture?

In that last, poignant hug,
Do you sense the weight of every shared day,
Or do you wish for a quicker end,
To let the memory drift away?

www.ingramcontent.com/pod-product-compliance
Lightning Source LLC
LaVergne TN
LVHW010838200726
843508LV00012B/2651